outlier

outlier

walter hildebrandt

Ekstasis Editions

Canadian Cataloguing in Publication Data

Hildebrandt, Walter
        Outlier

        Poems
        ISBN 1-896860-20-6

        1. Alberta--History--Poetry. 2. Saskatchewan--History--
Poetry. I. Title.
        PS8565.I4335O98   1998   C811'.54   C98-910968-X
        PR9199.3.H475O98   1998

Author Photo: Peter Tittenberger

Acknowledgement:
Some of these poems have appeared in *City Magazine; Prairie Journal Trust, Nashwaak Review'; Vintage 91: Prize-winning Poems from the League of Canadian Poets*, Sono Nis Press, 1992; and *Heading Out: The New Saskatchewan Poets*, Coteau Books, 1986.

I would like to thank Don Kerr, George Melnyk , Charles Noble and Richard Harrison for their advice and comments on poems in this book.

Published in 1998 by:
Ekstasis Editions Canada Ltd
Box 8474, Main Postal Outlet
Victoria, B.C., V8W 3S1

Ekstasis Editions
Box 571
Banff, Alberta T0L 0C0

THE CANADA COUNCIL | LE CONSEIL DES ARTS
FOR THE ARTS | DU CANADA
SINCE 1957 | DEPUIS 1957

Outlier has been published with the assistance of grants from the Canada Council and the Cultural Services Branch of British Columbia.

For Sarah and Mary
with me along the way

Contents

The Same Old News

When a man has his mouth so full of food that he is prevented from eating, and is likely to starve in consequence, does giving him food consist in stuffing still more of it in his mouth, or does it consist in taking some of it away, so that he can eat?

Soren Kierkegaard
Concluding Unscientific Postscript

It's history

they

're

taking

from

us

with

all

the   ir

con

fess   ionals

on

the

eve

ning

news

And so when a man has much knowledge, and his knowledge has little or no significance for him, does a rational communication consist in giving him more knowledge, even supposing that he is loud in his insistence that this is what he needs, or does it not rather consist in taking some of it away?

S.K.

in this long thin land
it's our place

they

              're

in

              vading

with

              flashes

blurring

past

destroy

              i

              n

              g

our

connections

                              g
                         n
                    i
               v
          i
g
u
s
          (h)
            o
            u
      their
            daily
                              luring
                         e
                    r
               u
            t
       u
f

still

passed by

a few

pro

      gress

di   i

        n

        g

        s

        e

      non

        s

        e

re

      turning

dis

      order

sense

                              e

                        c

                  a

            p

s

                  time

                              there

                              their

                              they-re [in]-place

(demanding)
                    control
returning order
amnesia spreads
                    a /
history
                    b /
unk
          now
                    n
And
          we
                    're
to believe
It's just
one damn
thing
after an
other

Outlier

On this paved road
I drive
to the hills again
Deer cross the road
On the post an owl
A distant coyote
moves
behind barbed wire
          The ever
                    circling hawk

Here wolfers
sodden drunk
swept like thirsty fire
across an Assiniboine camp
in some mistaken revenge

Solomon and Farwell
came here to take what
they could from this
now dying buffalo land
where poisoned carcasses
enticed wolves
          with their worn beauty.

Strange, tall lodge pole woods stand above
rich green grasses that spread across last year's wallows
renewed from a warm earth
once fire fed
and the dark
scorched earth returned
this light spring cover

Fort Battleford's History

The new men of the Empire are the ones who believe in fresh starts, new chapters, clean pages; I struggle on with the old story, hoping that before it is finished it will reveal to me why it was that I thought it worth the trouble.

J.M. Coetzee

I drive each year
to Fort Battleford
to tell guides
the history that has made it
a site of national significance

Most don't know what the Cree tell
believing what is written:
that the history
of the fort is honourable
its significance captured
in the grand architecture
of the Gothic Revival details
on the Commanding Officer's Residence

The full history
lies in the stories
that remain
untold
of the eight Indians
hanged within the
stockaded fort
now lying
next to the
Battle River
underneath an unmarked
slab of cement
surrounded
by a metal chain

history
that will not
tell their story
historians who
write about the
past so their sons
can live
comfortably with it

We read about the good intentions of
Christian people yet
little of the starvation
Big Bear knew and spoke
few listened

A hundred years later
I drink in a bar divided
have spent the day
explaining you cannot
rely totally
on what
has been
written

Tomorrow
I will
take them down
to the
common
grave
along the
river bank
beyond
the police
fort
in the beautiful
gully
where
the hillside
levels off
to the water
where
the concrete
slab
lies
unmarked

Winnipeg

You re-enter this city
    on tracks
                          cold and hard
      deer
          hooves
      breaking thru
          a razor thin crust
      narrowing
          towards the fading
               horizon
      fence posts
chain linked
          and barbed
      strung north
      penetrate
               the heart of the city
        over
            rib cages
              strewn
              throughout woods
An iron hard steel rail hums
      (y)our first music
            broken
      distant
           hooo hoo
              whoo
                who
                  ooo

Old Winnipeg

Peripatetic
    Windswept tanned hailed and rained on
The old man
combs the streets
in an old long black heavy dirty woollen coat
summer and winter
he sleeps everywhere
his tangled matted beard
now grizzled with frost
icicled by the breeze funneled down Portage

Bent under the coat (he's never without)
he hoards warmth
lives of the single
men who got off at the station
over the years
returns
where the train stopped
to let them out
stepping onto Main
to the North End
labourers at odd jobs
cleaning building city streets
hands calloused from hammer pick and shovel
    he says little
wanders the downtown streets
some evenings
he's on the Perimeter
walking monotonously like Harry Dean Stanton in Paris, Texas

He's rough balding
passers-by avoid him
he asks for money now and again
ever so politely
hardly bothers
anyone
downtown
in the old
Aberdeen
he drinks his draft slowly, carefully

remembers the crossing
and his mother's old country
cabbage soups
inside
his dream

Late Afternoon Walk

                    and after the game
from behind the Deaf School
                    across the fields of flocking birds
            I'll come by
                                  your place
                    to walk
                                  by the river

watch smooth grey water still flow to the bridge
                    listen to the dry rustle soothe this fall air
        lie down on moist layers
                          of golden pear shaped leaves
        light
                falling
                        wet
                                      and warm
            rising

                          in poplar scent
                                          surrounded

Waiting

I move
to the knowledge
of an unravelling
slow and deliberate
away from
the centre
where too
much is layered, marked

Where the childlike rock
for comfort
where sparrows
drive away the hawks
where a bit further
from the din of traffic
we will wrap our
baby in
a soft blanket
woven by old
Indian women
whose quills
leave no trace
drawing the
sparkling silver
thread brought
by swallows
from high in the trees
in this we will
take our baby
by an autumn
dawn
on a dew gilded carpet
through shimmering aspens
to where two rivers meet

and there watch the quiet flow
we will be attentive by twilight
before the city moves to
whatever lies at the edge of the mind
where the crepe-papered
wisps of feathery white mist
            turn with the golden fall leaves.

November Ditch

In summer

the fields were blocks of
managed color — from bright mustard to steel blue flax

Now the fields are black —

machine furrowed and

the ditches

once green or mowed
come alive
pale weaving colours
dance in the sun -
above an old seeder
rust and muted brown
play in a pure cool light
greyed weeds bow
amid the scattering white fluff of cattails
and waiving yellowed grasses
sway with the breeze
before the iron hard cold
and the cover of a rain silvered snow

General Hospital

Foucault
        is in the halls of the General Hospital
        his eyes are everywhere cannot rest
        we are subjects
        becoming
            no one

Gregor Samsa
        is here too
        somewhere
        trying to get out
          F. would like to help

We are here for inscription
        waiting for a birthday
           and naming

The hospital is clean — very clean
The rooms pleasant — too pleasant, comfortable
                "Relax"

There are lines on the floor
To tell us where to go
        Gregor follows them
There are uniforms and rules
To help us know what to do
Where and when to move

In the birth room
There is no one in charge
The shift changes
Now there is someone new
Questions are not welcome
There is a large clock on the wall
We keep time

Like us Gregor is quiet just now
He is on the floor — in the dark

The Machines cannot monitor
Our child's heartbeat
                                        they're useless

Sarah's water has not broken
There is no progress

We ask why they do not break the
                                        membrane

We are told only a doctor can
I ask for a doctor to break the water
We are told that the doctor
Will not come til birth is imminent
We are hours away
No one can decide

Laws turn form in different ways
The shift changes
The hand moves

The power is there but no one has it
This is how it works

I pace the halls
Where there are many rooms

DO NOT ENTER
I am sure Gregor is in the one
            at the end of the hall
I heard the ticking of his feet
            on the shiny hard waxed floors
His time is nearly up

On leaving
The desk tells us
          we do not fill out the forms properly
None of us

          do
                    Who can

This is where we begin — all of us

Outside the air is finally clear
                    Only Quiet

Mary's Birthday

A sole Red Impatiens
against the grey clapboards
the last budding brightness of this early fall

From the warm
           delicate
                note
                    high and fragile
Distant

The exotic perfumed Mexican parrot
Eyes
A night flight of the Snowy Owl
Away from the Magpie's thieving squawk

Take for now
the shelter
bent over you
Use our site
to view the world

From the first tremble

Swim in the fluid swirling motion
        of thin
            flamingo pink . . .
                    smoked glass
By rainbows
        Summer's Glads

On a magic carpet
        white dolphins
           leaping

My Living Room Window

There's something behind it still
the haloed painter's brush on one pane
inside scattered bits of color
outside a petunia blend
by the window
a Flin Flon miner, a curler, Prairie Duster,
the rock pile, late summer sunflowers —
not all of an elm trunk
cut-off in the window,
quartered,
yet lighter - brighter,
just part of a church,
a garage, fences, a piece of a house
in one corner
and grouped kids going home from school
inside and close bouquets of dry
greyed grasses, browned dock weed,
sage and wheat,
against the distant outside green.
The just yellowing leaves
the frenzied time of
first classes
foreign texts
frames
eastern voices
told us about
the railway and quarter-sectioned
fields of grain.
Full
after northern summers
we returned from
the loons' night calls and
the pelicans' white flight over
quiet cold deep-blue diamond-flecked waters
back from ball tournaments
in dusty small towns
where we drank "Boh"

Hangings

The old tapestries
show a
finely crafted history

layer on layer
year after year
a privileged
contact
with the past —

                  historians who
                  wrote for a few

Old hangings warmed cold damp castles
Green trees hide a serpent's shaded path

Lower Creighton
these were not
histories of a country
but of a nation
conceived in old boys' clubs
for business
read and carefully studied
at private colleges
where the tapestries hung
by the stage
for a people they all knew

who to serve?

Disney World and Johnny Cash
looked better and more believable
to West-siders, Northenders,
Indians of God's Lake
Icelanders of the Interlake
Métis of Round Prairie
Their own stories told in pubs

                       not written
Where 50's Coke signs hang with stuffed
                  moose heads

Payp, Payp

breaks
the automatonic
motion
of pedestrian traffic
as the paperman
with
his tobacco
stained
moustache
and
ragged dirty
clothes
sits at
the Vaughan Street
entrance
of the
Bay to
bark his
presence
he offends and
frightens
those who
do not
expect him
or know
that far from
being hunched
harmlessly
on his chair

he reminds
them
how thin
the surface is —
where
print ink
bleeds
across lines
blotches
stand out
"PAYP" "PAYP"
"paper lady?"
"paper sir?"

To the Market Gardener's

The old lady
washes
her hands covered
by thick wet mud

looks up
as we walk
to the wooden
stand
protected by canvas
We drive here
North
on the Henderson Highway
to buy
fresh carrots, onions
squash, potatoes
tomatoes deep red fully ripe
I was here
a year ago
just after
Mary was born
The Glads
then as now were in
full bloom
have been cut
some customers pick
simple white and red arrangements
others the exotic purple, orange
yellow with red spots sprayed
out towards the edges
on the beam
above us
along with some Glads
at 3

The old lady
with a distinct
eastern European accent
looks
with her deep blue eyes
at Mary
who becomes
quiet
in my arms
as the old lady begins
to talk
she wears
a long cotton print dress
buttoned over her large front
and an old dark blue sweater
hangs open
it is late evening
almost closing
she talks about her children
her dead husband
then turning
dips into the muddy
cold water in the pail
says that Mary
will like mud too
as she rubs
her thick rough
peasant hands
she suddenly straightens
smiles at Mary
the lines running
to her eyes and mouth
deepen
tells us
she talked to a couple
some days ago

who had no children
who didn't want any

she says loudly
throwing up her hands
"children are everything"
as her daughter busily
packs our vegetables
into an old paper bag
"You got to leave something behind
what else is dere
Romeo's not gonna help you
when you get old"
You got to leave
some
thing be
hind
"Dere is noting
                    else"
"you got to leave something behind"
she turns
in the dimming light
bends
and reaches for a towel

Sundance
after Bill Lobchuk's print

Over
winter's thin
greying garments stretches
a spring sky

a negative
            scratched
into life

Under
tattered rotting fringes
the warm land
                stirs

a full-breasted
woman

        languidly
        arches
towards heavens

        on fire

Late Recognition

a glaze
        rose red still hangs
                above growing drifts
piercing
           white
                    sheet crusts
yellow
           drops caught
       in ice covered
                          rows of
          marigold
                      slivers

Among Shadows

Just now
      sunlight
warms the last of Sarah's
                summer flowers
        those just fading
                    colors
   It's before the stalks
               brittle

                  dry   snap
and the earth slows
        leaves gaping cracks

        times

          to recall these
      bright shades
               wild flowers
        drooping galardia
      deep red begonia
at dawn
   still
     morning glory
        sky blue

After Work Drinking

There's not much
difference
down here
in the dark
log walled
Aberdeen
between the young guys drinking fast arguing after
work with just one more for the road
and the old guys
with yellowing grey
hair or the too black Maurice Richard look
red eyes drooping and
deeply
lined skin
drinking
slowly
they're sometimes silent for a long time
talk
when no one
appears
to be
listening

Biking to Work

I keep looking
for an easier passage
on the way through
the rough part
of the West End

In the afternoons
men sit on the front stairs
mothers here are
Indian, Filipino, Viet Namese

I try
to get across
main arteries
busy with traffic
to and from
the suburbs

St. Matthew's, Sargent, Wellington, Notre Dame
more recent signs
Only Portage and Ellice a
way out
once
for ancestors
traders, hunters, provisioners
tripmen going through to Carlton
Edmonton
the Peace River country
At the Women's Pavilion
a safe passage
a cross
walk
the final Xing
on Portage near Main
where I ride
over
the wide
white bars
on the street

Lake of the Woods

The wealthy line the shores of this lake
And with their friends own the (I)slands
Fishing flights for the fat ones to the north
They come back loaded
you hear them get off from the other end of town
A man from Kentucky owns the fish locker
We ask for pickerel. He sells us
"walleye" with a filleting knife in his back pocket
On leaving he smiles. Says
"yieuw awl kum bayk now"
North Dakotans own the cabins we're in
They're immaculately clean. Call them "camps"
At night playing pool we meet the hostess
She is very gracious. Speaks with a slight accent
She's from Grand Forks
Next day we ask what all the noise was across the lake
"Just Indians"
Says the woman, "probably shooting ducks"
It's getting late
Rent the canoe to see rock paintings
Oil from motor boats laps the shore
There isn't much time
The wind picks up algae collects in
The bays and suds
From detergent begins
To show

Winnipeg

Again tonight Russell leaves
the hotel
nothing is clear
his roots somewhere
among the northern miners
most don't believe
he knows what he's talking about
content will burst the form
it's so cold out
      sheer ice
he falls breaks ribs
the cage on the right aches

he leans into the harsh winds
horse hooves echo
the world is blurred
further on he falls
          again
on his way
to the north
he won't know how bad it is til morning
but when he reaches home
a few things become illuminated
the artwork he saw in the window
on his way thru the old warehouse district
makes it all clear
among the exhaust
that stays close to the ground
some things are becoming
so focused
he can't wait to make it
to Burrows
marching past the homes of the strike leaders
the fallen on main street
late at night
where the pain is distant
          numb

he writes
that the forms can't hold
now he remembers
writes what no one will say
what has been forgotten
about what happened
when the gunfire ripped
flesh lead lodged in bone
by morning all this is lost
again as fire
destroys the side
that housed the stories
that were put down

Ottawa 1988

The man sitting
on the concrete
wall
in the Sparks Street Mall
is clearly
broke
    n
he asks
the noon crowd

                              "Any change?"

the words
    drop
         falling
      apart
             as they hit
          rock bottom

Power Box
after Kelly Clark's drawing

Light
switches

Power
Coils
from the main beam
of the old
wooden warehouse

currents
coming and going
                    from
real power
                    outside
main cables re
lay
          c
        criss
          o
          s
          s
     crowding
          n
          g

power spreads
                    anonymously

Wires
        plugs
glass-eyed
        fuses
juice thru copper
aluminum-steel
alloys

Breakers automatic
        for overloads
                power-tools
                        sewing machines

lined up in sweatshops below

filipino ladies
        working
                inside
                beside
                        daughters
                                without
                                        complaint

Portage at Main

(after the charge)

In   the   tall

computer   card

office   towers

descendants

of   the   committee

proliferate

dominate

city   hall

since 1919

it's   been a   corporate

agenda

goal   oriented   optimistic

trading   inside

manage   grain   market

interest   consumers   bank

outwit   manipulate   credit

exclusive   clubs   school

stock   exchange

rate

market   research

organize   cost

free   enterprise

cutting   wages

gov't   control   use

purse strings   value

tied   tight   gold

standard   net   work   turn

over   change   evaluate   land

grab   venture   tax   cuts

billable   hours

real   private   property   incentive

trickle   down   middle

management   high

interest   class   transactions

family   hierarchy   bonds

dependent   father

stocks   absent   mother   float

deal   dice

throws   out   pay

competitive   background   bonus

business

history

formal   customers

money   decisive   chairman

nurture   protection

bypass   grants   escape   capital

bankruptcy   sales

sponsors   safety   nets

bail   out

office   hours   control

board   secretaries   ownership

run   late

interest   class   transactions

leverage   risk   technology

profit

network   fund

capital   manipulate

slush   corporate   client

change   political   savvy

kick-back   system   advances

analytical   skill

competitive   world

oriented

stake   holders

the bottom line...

profit   margin

marketing   downsize

accountability

progress...

National Gallery 1988

At the new
National
Gallery
art
can not be
safe
guards
everywhere
the uniform
in contemporary
Can. art

a man in blue
phase
orders me
away
from Favro's
fake river
it *must* be viewed from a distance

       the sign
       says
       Serra's plate
       can not be
       touched
       is finely
       balanced

and
a note
to the sticker
beside
Hans Haacke's
Alcan
works

to say
the company
sold out
its interest
in South African
mines
in 1986
news
changes art
image of
Steve Biko's
stitched up
body
remains

words say
company
altered
policy
art shows
this
made money

Chicago 1989

I think back

        a lot about the public library

   such a grand monument

           to victory

                  remains

          marble columns

    gold gilding

       commemorating

    this horrible prelude

   to Great War

      500,000 dead

stays with me

            long after

   Benjamin was right

       documenting barbarism

Sherrie Levine,

    among the most radical

             of today's

        appropriating

artists,

        redoes

          the work of master

       photographers

and painters

       which she then signs as her own,

     thereby expressing

        her Postmodern

           skepticism

regarding the possibility and relevance of orginality

              in art today.

By removing the image from the object...

           da

              da

                da

                  da

But

    we didn't see

                        the Seurat

when we went

        to the Chicago Art Institute

Well

     we just

          didn't get

            around to it

  so much

       excess

          arti

            facts

from civilizations

        now hon
           oured

 by these American

       connoisseurs

almost lost our knapsack

Guy with jack-boots

       airport waiting room

   says "they got shit

          for security
              here"

    at O'Hare

"no wonder
         we get the fuck blown out of us"

   these are big guys

      ZOG guys

        tough guys

it's a well dressed

      man
        hustles

   us for a limo at the airport

Mechanical reproductions

On the Art of Fixing a Shadow

        photo show
        photo collection
        photo display

And
      in comment book

you don't state
anywhere
photography reinforces
proliferates 17th century
autonomous
Newtonian Carestian individual
against
older sense of community
medieval

      art's photos better
          at
            Museum of Contemporary Art

At Dick's Last Resort

    printed
               on waiters' T-shirt

            :
    Don't ask what

             Dick can do

      for you

  Ask

      what you can do

  for Dick

At

        basketball game

     Chicago : Boston

       Jordan
             flies

   Bird

        wins it

      with last shot

Guy

      in the art gallery

    restaurant

     asks

        where the ketchup is?

  surly waitress

       says: "It's on the table."

  Guy says

    "That's just the way I like it ma'm"

Jordanian cab driver
   studies
         accounting

     drives me to Chicago Stadium

       thru slums

   says he's going back

         too crazy here

still better than NY he says

     says customers
           surprized

      he wants to go back

    think he's lucky
          to be alive

       so much violence
            (t)here

   says in 5 years

      still hasn't met

        his landlord

    everything done over phone

New Orleans piano

　　　　　　　　　　player

　　　playing

　　　　　　　　lovers

　　　　at bar

　　　　　　　　　stealing

　　　　a kiss

　　　　　　　　against

　　　　the system

　　　　　　　　　jazz

traffic

　　　　　　pavement

　　bike

　　　　　riders

　　　suicide

　　　　　　　mission

　　against

　　　　　the flow

official

      history

    sanitizes
          war
   appropriates
          absorbs
              every
                thing

    the black

  Carbide
        building
     stands out
         polished

      by cheap
           wages
Newberry Library

   whites

        studying

Native History

    a system

designed

     to stifle

   criticism   intellectuals

     universities

    get the job done

63

Hefner's

      once
         grand

   Playboy Club

         dominates

   sterile deli

       white bunnies
       black waiters

Says there's a giant on the beach

        sees Gulliver
            from Days Inn

Chicago
Chicago
       it's my kinda town

Mary likes the Indian Pow-Wow on the wharf

       listens dances
           to the drums

Weeks later
     in Winnipeg

   asked where she was born

   says Chicago

   remembers the Pow-Wow

Toll

Bells toll every 15 min.

here

where the British accent is still in

here

where experts in history are

theologians

just over there

down the hall

no students

here

where the economics expert

tells students

that the poor

are poor partly

by accident and

partly

through their own fault

its Christian eeconomics (they're told)

Bells toll every 15 min.

                              here

            where everyone wants

                  attention

      where there is no youth

      where sherry is taken

                  on Friday afternoons

here

where there's so much

                        sadness

                  to be away from the old

                              country

            it's dreary

here   azaleas droop

            it smells

            like old wax

      lawns unwatered

            that dull

            Church

                  feeling

The bells toll every 15 min.

                                        here

        where arrogance is refined

here

        where they're

                                undoing

    "all the damage done by the Marxists"

here

        where energy is slowed

            by taunting

                        daring

The bells toll every 15 min.

                                    here

          where radicals

                                drink

                fawned over

                    by youthful

                                    ambitious admirers

          told how art can make money

The bells toll every 15 min.

                                             here

                  where the radical

                                 is inaccessible

                                 is academic

                                                    is

                                 no threat

here

        where the tories wait

            where the tories control

                where the tories watch

                    where the tories sleep

                        where the tories need not discuss

The bells toll again

　　　　　　it's 15 min.

　　　　　　　　past

　　the world

　　　　goes on and on

　　with the inconsequence

　　　　of a foreign

　　　　　　　　university

　　where middle-aged

　　　　mature students

　　are encouraged

　　to say

　　　　　what's on their minds

The bells toll at

                                        quarter to

                the hour is getting

                                                    late

                here

                where they wait for spring

                            to get away

        a love so desperate   distant

                here

                    in these crummy dusty

                                        offices

The bells toll on the hour

                              here

          where the old won't leave

       where the new goes around

               and around

         where Christianity

            is a sorry whisper

          smells of moth balls

                   chrysanthemums

The bells toll every 15 min.

                                             here

                to interrupt

                            uxurious

        talk

                        love   behind

                                              closed doors

              a foreign

                      student

                humiliated

                  "Do you understand English?"

this is where it all ends

                  for many

                who need to know

      here

              where the bells toll

                          so often

    amid sighs

The bells toll half past

the hour

where silence

works

on those who are only slightly

timid

where the confident say little

where ideas

threaten

where the powerless stay silent

screams

nightmares

where the bankrupt get

promoted

minorities

        are hard to find

Americans

       dominate

              the art department

the blonde blue-eyed research

           sensation

    explains

   why the Métis

      have no land claims

    for the gov't rate of $500 a day

   this is how it works

The bells toll every 15 min.

                         here

      where there's so painfully little

           to say

      here where intellectuals tell

           students

           theory is dead

           pragmatism is in

           in Thatcher's Britain

Here

      where the radical

           waits

           reduced

      to shameless self-indulgence

Here

      from the now empty

           office

           where

           the bells still

           toll

Into Montana

We travel backwards
along the way
the Nez Perce took
to escape the U.S. Army

down through strange hoo doo formations
a language in ochre on rocks
Writing-on-Stone
            sacred
in distant haze the Bears Paws' rise

across the line
backdrop to this land the spirits walk
by campers picnic tables and RVs

The rough gravel road to Fort Benton in decline
since rail replaced water
where traders took supplies
north to prairie tribes
displaced by starvation slaughter bullets and whiskey
                                    poisoning
a land of rhythms and cycles

South across the Judith Basin
breaks where Sitting Bull's victorious tribe
left the Little Big Horn for Canada
the land of their 1812 ally the Queen

Land marked by sites
signs telling travellers the story
of the non-treaty Nez Perce
from Idaho across mountains to Yellowstone
battles along the way, 1877
Cottonwood (July 4-5) Clearwater (July11-12)
Fort Fizzle (July 25-28) White Bird
Canyon (June 17) Big Hole (Aug. 9)
Camas Meadows (Aug. 20) Canyon Creek (Sept. 3)
Cow Island (Sept. 23) Bear Paw (Sept. 30-Oct. 5)
                         and White Bird north to Canada
Passed geysers and stinking mud pots
the Nez Perce with women and children
outran the U.S. Army
victories and standoffs

Helena built on gold and glory
boutiques in the small red brick hovels
Reeder's Alley
homes of the miners scratching
for a chance
where the Chinese worked day and night
across the way secretly mining while their bosses slept

Bannack the short lived capital
the Nez Perce skirted

North for a night in Hamilton
the Montana Militia threaten the local
justice of the peace declaring unconstitutional
her conviction of a militia member for a parking ticket
they have their own justice their own system
their own laws
survivalists

And Missoula trout fishing and fire jumpers
Californians are arriving
escaping earth quakes and mudslides
along fault lines to the west

North again to Canada
miles to the west of where White Bird
took the last of the free Nez Perce
to Sitting Bull's camp at Wood Mountain
Suknaski's place

A few of these Lakota and Nez Perce
are still among us
Chief Joseph and the ones who stayed
were betrayed kept out of their homelands
died of malaria diseases they had no
resistance to
                escape
        dreams of
                high passes and cool river valleys
running from
                the Continental Divide
        the Bitterroot
                sacred to the Nez Perce
                                Medicine Men

P.A. Boys

Tiger tells
          how
      this moonias woman
                    came
to his table
              in the bar
        asked if he remembered
                              her
          he says "No"
                    (in Cree)
        she asks him why he's speaking Cree
                                          winks
            she says he slept with her
                      smiles
              and lifts her dress a little
                              scares him
          so he had to leave
                        the bar
      eyes
              sparkling

by now he's talking English
          to the boys in
                      the Mall
which he does when he's had a couple

over 80
          he still jumps
                    lightly

            making hardly

                    a sound

81

Edgar Mapletoft, Frenchman Butte, May 1991

Edgar and I exchange books
when I arrive
"you've got to give to get,"
says Edgar as he hands me
the book about women on the Thunderchild reserve
"whites have little idea of what they've
done to the Indians here"

Edgar knows a lot
about the Cree
around here
local Cree chiefs
were pall bearers
at his wife's funeral
he proudly says
Cree boys stayed
with them and went
to school from Edgar's home
his cattle graze on
the lands of the Cree
on the nearby reserve

It's one of the few places
the Cree and locals get along so well
Cree families attend
the local dinner here tonight
to honour Lloyd Furman
who took care
of the museum til his death earlier this year
It's a country extravaganza
local singers
local plays put on
stories about the

brothers who lived
in a cave
along the river bank
after their military service
politicians attend (both PC and NDP)
Cree dancers start the evening
Edgar finishes the evening
with what he says is a Native dance
a jig
from a video of Métis dancing

he said he was a little bit nervous
since it was the first time
he performed it in public
brought along his own piece of plywood to dance on

Edgar's proud of the history here
The history of the local Indians
"We've got alotta history here"
he has lectured about Big Bear
at Lac La Ronge
he has given many guided tours
of Frenchman Butte, Steele's Narrows
Fort Pitt, Frog Lake, Loon Lake
he knows a lot
values the friendship
of the elders still living
Jimmy Chief, Jimmy Canepotatoe
who joke and laugh with Edgar

This is a strange country
where Big Bear protected the white women
where the Mann's were loved by
the local Cree
Seekaskootch shot
by one of his own people
the Hutterites
get along with the locals here

Back at the museum
Edgar talks about his plans
big plans
Edgar says he'd eventually hold
seminars so that people
could come out and learn about
this place
After the long dinner
Edgar and I
go for a beer
at the Valley View Bar
There is a band
of young Cree
singing rock and country
songs
They finish with
Ghost Riders in the Sky
Edgar loves the music
he claps
Hurrays
at the end of the songs
the locals all greet him
as they pass by the table

Edgar says he feels like the Cree
about the land
could never leave it
says he misses his wife terribly
he says
he never knew
he would miss her so much
tells me I probably think
he's crazy as a bed bug
says he sometimes dances
by himself at night
says he loves to dance
he's afraid to stop
it's a love that keeps him going

Edgar keeps busy
doesn't like TV
wants me to send him stuff
on Theresa Delaney and Theresa Gowanlock
wants to know more about them

In the morning
Edgar takes me to the place
where he believes Middleton
disembarked
for his advance against the Cree
we find bully beef
tins scattered all over flats
just up from the river
its likely a spot
unknown
to others til now

November/Whales

for Sarah

A thaw
followed
then cold set in
for some days after
the first heavy snows

      Finally
      cold enough
      to take and hold this
      conglomerate
      form
      just pebbles left
      covering
      ice beneath
      stones both
      absorbing and
      reflecting a grey
      sunlight
      not warmth enough
      remaining
      to melt right down
      just yet

these odd traces
drawing eyes
to the dull pale
still green lawn
dotted by
freakish
crazy little
hoo doo shapes

And Greene
feared
dissipation
talk
        destroying
losing out
to boredom
                again
resistance
        a cover
        no one
        to find
        out
to escape
crowding drowning beneath
the just thick
enough surface
bloodied battered mouths
frustrated
knowledge leads
to some air
hole
thrashing in desperation
the circle (deceit) closing in
now each
square
cut by chain saws
Inuit hunters
lead up to
open water

holes
smashed
helicopters
huge balls iron
i.e. wrecking machines
breaking ice
dropping

some reporters said when
          freed
from the ice packs
          feared
they wouldn't go south
would grow attached to
frantic rescuers
working to
free them

darkening days
against whitening land
Inuit
watch bears
chased away
choppers
follow these strange disappearances
In the past
at early freeze-up
some whales would die

Bizarre
man-made paths
across a settling silence
holes smashed
by desperate men
Inuit and
white seeing little
of the other
ice-breakers leave
a jagged trail
bills will be paid
in Europe and North America
whites will pay

leaving the leading trail
dreaming later
drifting
muscle bound
chest and biceps
tight
frozen stiff
a ball point
pen thawing
names across
the flat wall of a slowly turning
ice-berg buoyed up by the massive still life below
some strewn words
frozen solid
in the long dark
melting
pieces slip away distant
in random collisions
floating

and later
in the fall
of acid eaten trees
she found
me cut by square
stone bruised
barely
breathing
beside these odd
now recognizable markers
of nature
close to
the cemetery
I could never find before
bleeding staring
at a dim sky
darkened by chevrons
of late departing geese
lying there
slowly chewing black
just turned leaves

in this
bitter sweet
season too heavy
for love songs
trying to get in
death haunts
reeds mark
a lower sun
yet even in cooling marshes
and in take-off
beating wings lift
scattering white among
these once solemn sentinels
but for us
it all ends up
holding
you holding me
grey whales
heading south

In the cool late August light
  Our porcelain blue Morning Glories last
    Far into the afternoon

Notes

"Boh" on page 31 refers to the brand of beer "Bohemian" that used to be brewed in Prince Albert.

"P.A." on page 82 refers to the Saskatchewan city of Prince Albert.

Printed in April 1998 by

in Boucherville, Quebec